The *Wise Woman's* Academy®

C.F.O. TRAINING

The Wise Teen's Guide
To Financial Facts &
Entrepreneurial Basics

JJ Nocco

Welcome to the Future – Your Financial Future.

Get Ready to become a Financial Whiz and Entrepreneur while still in Middle or High School. Here you will learn Financial Facts about Money and Saving Money that will give you advantages all thru your life. You will also learn Entrepreneurial skills to maximize the Tools and Apps you already have at your fingertips but are not maximizing to your advantage YET.

Not only will these Financial Budgeting Skills put Smart Money Power in your life now but will allow you to have more money control at every pivot point in your life as you grow up.

These Skills will allow you to plan your purchases and discipline your spending to prevent impulse buying habits that usually keep us broke and in debt.

These Skills will train you on How to have Your Ideal Life sooner, at an earlier age, rather than later or never.

Additional Entrepreneurial Skills, in this volume, will help you to build a Successful Home Based Business that will give you a tremendous advantage in the ability to expand your income generating skills, at this age, and build a part time business that can help fund your desires now and for the rest of your life.

Welcome to The Wise Woman's Academy & Financial Training for Life

Wicked

VICTORIAN

BOSTON

Robert Wilhelm

THE
History
PRESS

Published by The History Press
Charleston, SC
www.historypress.net

First published 2017

ISBN 9781540217233

Library of Congress Control Number: 2017934949

The Wise Teen's Guide to Financial Facts & Entrepreneurial Basics

© 2016

JJ Nocco

Published by:

The Wise Woman's Academy
13512 Studebaker Road
Norwalk, CA 90650

jjnoccoauthor@gmail.com

First Printing, 2017

Printed in the United State of America

ISBN-13: 978-1546455226
ISBN-10: 1546455221

Be True to You –
Success Training Book Series

JJ Nocco

Dedicated to the

Wise Women that Motivate & Inspire Me

My Daughters Olivia & Monica

&

My Mentor Helen Ramirez & Her Protégé Elena

&

to the Future Success

of All the Readers who are Shaping

their Futures with our Be True to You

Success Training Book Series

Contents

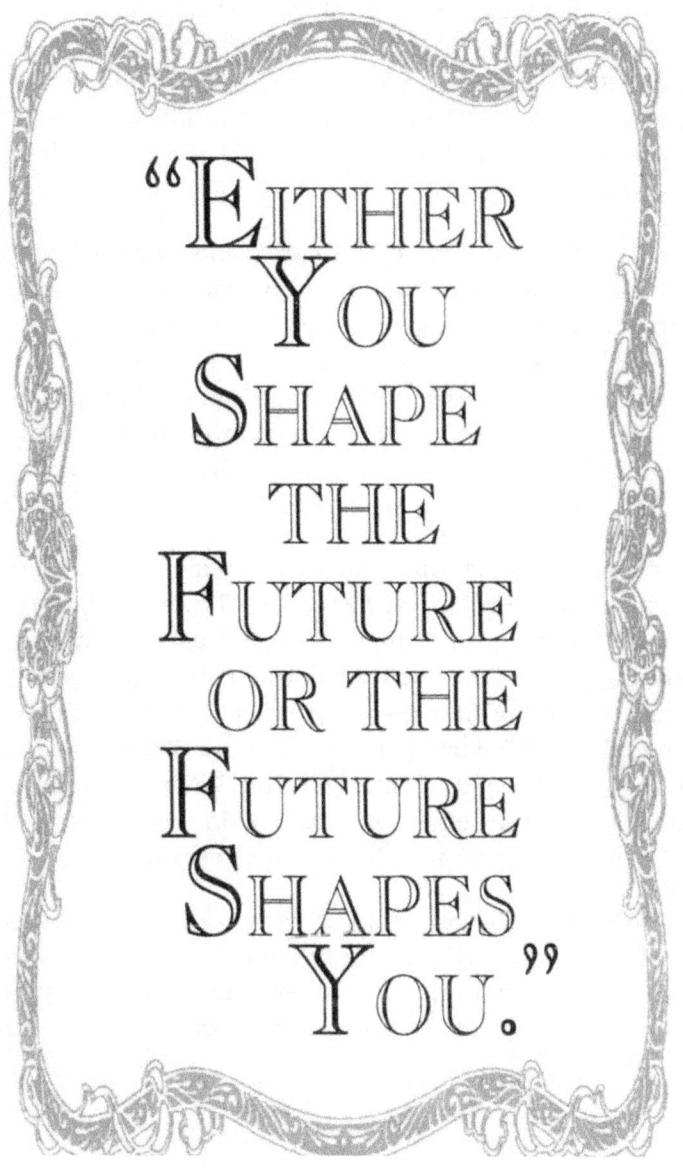

"EITHER YOU SHAPE THE FUTURE OR THE FUTURE SHAPES YOU."

Introduction

As a student you usually have limited income in the form of an allowance. Thru TV and all the advertising we are exposed to, it's no surprise that we are all influenced to be an "instant gratification society". No matter if we have $10.00, $100.00 or a $1,000.00 we want to go shopping but usually have a list of things to buy longer than our current funds. We spend it all now then we're broke and out of money till the next delivery of cash into our life.

Later in life, we'll have credit cards and handle them the same way. Spend it all, make minimum payments and look for another company to offer us a new card. This is how we get sucked into the "live beyond your means financial cycle" and owe all our weekly income to credit card payments and other bills and end up with no discretionary (free) funds left over for the extras we want in life. We can never get ahead financially because we're always in debt, and behind a payment or two.

Most young people will ruin their credit by age 25-30 or are already heavily in debt at that age. They will start their young adult life treading water financially and usually end up declaring bankruptcy to resolve the issues. Unfortunately, this is usually at the age where the first pivotal point in life occurs, the transition from childhood responsibilities to adult responsibilities, where you are usually getting married and having a family. With no credit, bad credit or a bankruptcy in your financial pocket, succeeding in this stage of life becomes very difficult.

You, however, will not have this experience because of the skills you will learn in this training manual. Your finances will always be under your control and money and credit will be a tool to having everything you want and not the other way around.

Start with Today

Ok let's start with your Now information.

Answer the following questions and write your answers here.

Name_____

Age _____

Year in School_____

Current Allowance _____

School Activities & Clubs_____

Hobbies _____

Family Members & Birthdays:

Dad_____

Mom_____

Brother _____

Sister _____

Grandma_____

Grandpa_____

Best Friends:

_____

Even at your young age, you can see you have a lot of activities and people in your life. School activities always require some cash for trips and other school events. Hobbies require supplies for your current project and it's usually not in the supplies that you already have. Families always have birthdays and special days and we usually want to give a little something special to the person being celebrated. Then there is Christmas where we wish we could rob a bank to be able to buy all those special things for the people on our list.

So let's get started and plan how to stretch your current money:

Fill in the Blanks from Your "Now Information"

- **My Allowance is:** _____
- **I Get It Every:** _____
- **The Total for the Month is:** _____

For example, you earn $10 a week from Mom doing house chores and earn $10.00 a week from Dad doing yard work.

Total for the week is $20.00 and we usually have 4 weeks a month,

so $20 x 4 = $80.00. Great – Let's go shopping right? WRONG!

We're going to learn budgeting, which in our case is also called disciplined gratification.

Let's start with setting up our Bank.

You'll need a zippered pencil pouch and 6 each of 9 ½ x 4 ¼ size envelopes.

1st Step:

Put the current year on the top left of your **1st** envelope and add the label "ME".

Put the current year on the top left of the **2nd** envelope and add the label "School & Hobbies".

Put the current year on the top left of the **3rd** envelope and add the label "Birthdays & Special Days".

Put the current year on the top left of the **4th** envelope and add the label "Christmas".

Save the other 2 envelopes for later.

This is a very good training bank. You can always add more envelopes if you have other important categories you want to allocate or save funds for. More details on this later.

2nd Step:

Turn the **1st** envelope the long way, like a sheet of paper, and write the numbers 1-20 from top to bottom, like a list. Now start writing down all the things you want for "ME".

No problem if you don't have 20 things right now. This bank is for the year and you will be crossing off the things you already bought and adding things you want to add to your list.

Take the **2nd** envelope and put the label "School" on top and add 10 lines. Then under #10 add the label "Hobbies" and add another 10 lines.

Now under the "School" Label write down the events you want to fund. Under the "Hobbies" write down the things you need for your current project.

If you can't think of any school or hobby things to list right now, no problem you can do it later as they come up.

11

You can also change the label of this envelope if school and hobbies don't apply to you. After all this is Your Bank!

Now the **3rd** envelope is tricky. On a piece of binder paper write down all the names and birthdays you have on your list on page 5 and alphabetize them by the month they take place in.

Then get a calendar you can write in and flip thru each month and write down any special days your family celebrates like Mother's Day, Father's Day, Parent's wedding anniversary or any special event coming up this current year.

On this envelope, instead of numbers you'll write the months from January to December but leave space.

If you have a lot of names and dates you can use both sides of the envelope.

Now under each month copy the name & date of any birthdays or any special days or events happening in that month from your calendar.

The **4th** envelope is easy. Just write number 1-20 and write down the names of family, friends and other people in your circle of life that you want to give a Christmas gift to.

Take the **5th** envelope and mark ME NOW – yes, you will have a mini money account for spending on pay day for a treat or something special from this **discretionary account**.

Remember **"discretionary"** means free from being committed or promised to another category like you're me, school, hobbies, birthday or your Christmas account.

Great – now you're ready to start banking:

Take you 4 envelopes and take your $80.00 and divide the money equally into each one. Now each envelope has a deposit of $20.00. From your "Me" envelope and take $5.00 and put it in your "Me

Now" envelope. Remember the dollars you are actually putting in each Savings Account depends on the Total you are getting on Pay Day.

Wonderful, now you have your Bank and you have your accounts. Now it's time for the Rules.

These are the Wise Teen's Banking Rules:

1. **DEPOSIT** cash when earned equally into each envelope and take ¼ of the Me deposit to put in the Me Now account.
2. **EVERY WEEK** you will **Not** Go Shopping – you will plan your spending. Go to your account envelopes and review your Me; School/Hobby; Special Days lists to decide what you really need to buy for next month's gifts and special projects.
3. **ONLY SHOP** one time a month for Me, Hobby and any birthdays or special days coming up next month. Look for sales and BOGO's (Buy One Get One) to get more.
4. Set up a new envelope if you decide you want to build funds for a new category.

These are the Rules and you must Promise to follow them.

Sign _____**Date** _____

Great – so far you've learned the most important things about Budgeting and Banking.

Now, let's look at your interest and current skills so we can start planning to build a mini-business that can earn you more cash after homework is done on school nights and on the weekends.

What Do You Like To Do

Pets - _____

Plants - _____

Baking - _____

Painting & Bling Work -_____

Photos -_____

_____

_____

Now that you have an idea of what you would like to do, let's explore how we can grow these skills to earn you extra cash.

We will also begin your Financial Training in this section thru the use of accounting terms and Financial Facts.

Pets

If you're a pet person and like dogs, you can develop a small business working with neighborhood pets with your parent's permission and supervision.

You can offer to **walk dogs daily** or several times a week. Offer clients a 15 - 20 minute walk. Stay within sight of your home, walk down the block, cross at the corner, come back on the other side and cross back. You can follow this loop several times. Or just go back and forth on the same side. Be a Good Citizen and carry your poop bags to pick up any pet donations along the way. Keep pets on a leash and under control at all times. Use a cloth muzzle if you need to and offer a treat when you return the pet home if ok with the owner.

And

You can offer to **wash and brush out the dogs** you already work on week days   on the weekend by appointment. In the summer, you can air dry dogs in a sunny pen, in the winter you need to dry with a hair blower. Allow up to 3 hours per appointment and only have one dog with you at a time to keep from having any dog personality problems.

Always do the Best Job possible with each dog so your client always comes back and your business keeps going and growing.

How to Start- Advertise- all businesses need to advertise their services.   Have Mom or Dad help you design a flyer with some clipart from Microsoft office. Include a 50% appointment deposit so clients know you're a serious business person and have allocated your time to their pet. **Also create a Google Voice Number which rings on your phone to use as your business**

number, not your personal cell phone number, so clients can call if they are running late or need to reschedule for another time. Request a 24 hour cancellation/ reschedule call on the flyer so you have time to book a replacement appointment.

Let your extended family and friends parents know that you are starting a Pet Washing Business and would like their support. Also look around at your neighbors and see who the pet owners are and take a flyer to them. Have Mom & Dad pass out flyers at work and church and collect 50% deposit in cash when the appointment is made. Verify your availability on your calendar.

Stay in control of your business- Use a calendar to write appointments as soon as you make them and don't take on more than you can handle. Plan your "Work Week" to maybe schedule to walk 1 dog after school every day , doesn't have to be the same dog every day, and schedule to wash 2 -3 dogs on Saturday. Only walk dogs living on your block – Stay Safe and in Sight of home.

Always Be Safe – never go into stranger's or anyone's house or be alone with an adult, man, woman or teenager.

For Wash Appointments -schedule a firm drop off time and a firm pick up time and have an adult with you to greet clients.

Balance of payment must be in cash, include the appointment deposit to the total fee being charged and give a receipt with your name and google number so they can contact you again if they loose the flyer.

You can include a grooming perk like a fragrance spritz of doggie perfume or holiday perk to reward your client like a doggie bandana or holiday bows. Add a little something so that you and your service stand out to the client. You can find bulk goodies at Oriental Express .com. Also take a close up picture of the owner & pet with your cell phone, so you can remember what they look like and file in your client book. Go to your client's page anytime you are talking to them and are scheduling another appointment.

Also ask to see the pet's current rabies record to make sure they are safe to handle and post the info on their client page. And make sure they are receiving flea/tick control products. You don't want to contaminate your work environment with fleas and have your other dogs take them home.

How to Price - Call your local pet grooming stores and get their prices for baths. Be specific in your questions – is there a price difference between small and large dogs? How about long hair and short hair? Adjust your prices to 25 – 30% less than theirs price - you are offering faster service for only 1 dog at a time but you are learning new skills and can raise your price a little every year or have a Tip Jar in plain sight and you may get an extra dollar. If you're really like this job and are good at handling dogs, later you can learn to groom and expand your services to include cuts.

Work Place

Every business requires a work space, water, electricity and towels so even though you are working at home, be a good citizen and plan to contribute some cash towards these expenses. Hopefully you have a laundry sink in a laundry room or garage to use for washing the dogs and a flat surface to dry them at your eye level.

Inventory Supplies- These are consumable supplies that get used up and need to be replaced.

You need dog shampoo, doggie perfume for a going home spritz and old towels to dry and Q-tips for carefully cleaning the edges of ears. You will also need a good brush, a matt tool and maybe a grooming glove for short hair dogs. Also get a Receipt Book & calendar for posting appointments. **For Client Perks** -Holiday give away items like summer bandanas or Christmas bows

Costing and Profits   -   This step is necessary with every business – if you don't know how much it costs to do the job, how do you know if you are making a profit and how much

profit are you making after deducting the costs? This is the formula,

Service fee-inventory-fixed costs = profit

Every bottle of shampoo is good for several washes. Divide the cost of the bottle by the reasonable number of washes you can get from the label. Work up a small dog, medium dog and large dog cost sheet. Figure out the shampoo **variance** - use less for small dogs and more for bigger dogs so determine the cost for each and post on your dog size cost sheet you will also use more if the dog has long hair. Drying time in the sun or being blow dried will vary by the dog's size and type of coat. Time the drying process for sun or blow dry and check the dog every 10 minutes and record the time. Record the brush out time if the dog has long hair and has knots or if you are just using the grooming mitt to polish the coat.

Following these steps will give you a cost amount for each step and a cost total for every dog you wash. By also having accurate time information for each dog you will know when you can have the dog picked up and the next delivered or are free to do other things.

You will have a Dog Wash Client Sheet for each dog you handle. These steps are **cost accounting steps** and will allow you to accurately calculate cost and profits. Don't forget to include **fixed costs** like a water charge and electricity charge for blow drying and a laundry charge portion on every dog even if you wash all the dirty towels together.

This is a sample of the Dog Wash Client Sheet:

Owner's Name_____   Contact Phone _____

Pet's Name_____   Breed_____ Size_____

Referred By _____

Shots to Date _____ Long Hair _____ Short Hair _____

Where do they usually get washed?_____ How Often _____

Apt date_____ Time _____ Price _____

Deposit Paid _____ Balance Due at Pick Up _____

Receipt # _____ Next Apt _____

Apt date_____ Time _____ Price _____

Deposit Paid _____ Balance Due at Pick Up _____

Receipt # _____ Next Apt _____

When you get paid, don't forget to pay your expenses – electricity, water and laundry then replace the cost of your inventory and Bank the Profit.

Pet Owners Love Pet Pictures! Offer them for extra profit!

Once you get going and are comfortable with pets and owners you can offer to take pet photos for Holidays and Special occasions of pets alone or with the owner on your cell phone. All cell phones have cameras and editing software included that you can do a lot with. Go to the photo section in the book to see on how to print out the photos. I use Snapfish.com and they offer a very comprehensive service and reasonable prices.

Buy a doggie costume for the holiday happening that month and take a few photos of the dog in costume before the owner comes by. Show the owner when they arrive and tell them you are offering a photo special 4 x 6 for $2.50, a 5 x 7 for $5.00 and a 8 x 10 for $7.50. Just remember dogs move a lot so you will take a lot of shots of the same dog just to get 2 or 3 good ones but the advantage of a cell phone is you can instantly see the photos and delete the bad ones and enhance the good ones to show your client.

This service is called **diversification** which means offering a related service to your business. **From walking dogs to walking and washing to offering holiday or special My Doggie & Me pictures**. Diversify for more profits from the same clients.

Always do your best and clients will refer others to you and you, as the business owner, will have the option to add them as a wash client or just as a photo client.

Go to the Cell Phone Photography section on page 42 for more details.

Financial Facts #1 – How Money Grows

You deposit your paycheck into your favorite bank and any excess you leave from month to month earns 0-1% interest. This is a **Fixed Account**. You already paid income tax on your funds when you earned them, and if your excess funds earn interest you will again get taxed on the gains via a 1099 at the end of the year.

At the Bank, your money grows like this:

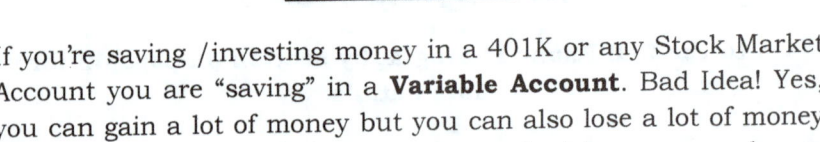

If you're saving /investing money in a 401K or any Stock Market Account you are "saving" in a **Variable Account**. Bad Idea! Yes, you can gain a lot of money but you can also lose a lot of money and may not have the earning years required to earn your losses back. You are also paying some company a management fee.

Most people "saving" in these accounts did not recover from 2008 losses before losing again in 2015 and again in early 2016. Many Financial professionals forecast 2016 losses to be equal to or greater than 2008. **See the Historical Performance Chart on page 55.**

In Variable Accounts, your money is doing this:

The **Best Way** to save securely is in an **Indexed Account usually called an IUL or GIUL.** These accounts have a "Floor" so you never lose your money, even in a bad year. They also have a "Ceiling" or CAP and it is always more than any bank product offers. **See the Historical Performance Chart on page 60.**

In an Indexed Account Your money is growing like this:

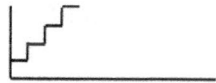

Indexed Accounts usually offer 8-12% Annual Interests with no losses. Later in this look we will look at how to use this type of account to your advantage.

Plants

If you like working with plants and watching them grow and bloom, you could build a little business from this interest. Most people like to have plants at home or in their office area but may not be very good at keeping them alive. This gives you an opportunity to build a little business offering plant replacement every 4 to 6 weeks.

Start with a trip to your local garden shop at Lowe's, Home Depot or your local garden shop and make a list of the following to get some ideas:

Look at the flower pony packs currently in the store's **inventory**. These are 4 or 6 packs of the same plant that is currently blooming at this time. A flowerpot of 3 kinds of flowers is a good design. Select a taller plant and 2  shorter plants of same or contrasting colors. Record the costs and use your cell phone to take pictures.

Look for the packages of plastic pot liners in about a 6" – 8" size and record the quantity per package and the cost.

Look at the 1 – 1 ½ cubic foot bag of Miracle Grow potting soil and record the cost. I like this brand for pots because it contains perlite to hold water and has plant food already mixed in.

Look for a small bag, ¼ to ½ cubic foot bag, of orchid bark to use for a top coat and record the cost.

Go home and use your collected information to calculate what you will offer and how much you will sell it for. Set up a **Cost Sheet** and call it "Flower Pot for (month)" list names of flowers used because plants will change while other supplies will stay the same.

Start with your pots, calculate a price for each one and post this on your cost sheet.

Look at the plant selection and decide on 3 plants per pot and divide the pony pack price by the individual plants to get a price per plant then add up the total for plants cost. Post on your cost sheet.

Determine how many pots you can fill from your bag of potting soil and get a cost per pot of soil and post on your cost sheet. Don't over fill your pot with soil, you need to top with the orchid bark and you don't want the pot to over flow when watered.

Estimate ½ cup of orchid bark per pot and calculate how many "toppings" you can get per bag. Post on your cost sheet.

Labor will just take a few minutes for shopping and for putting the pots together. Estimate 15 minutes per pot for both steps. You can set up an **assembly line process** and make the same arrangement at the same time depending on your plants. If your 3 plant selections have 6 plants each in their pony pack then you can make 6 pots assembly line style. If your plant selections have 4 in one and 6 in the others then you are limited to 4 pots assembled at a time.

Now that you have calculated all the component costs you can work up your "month pot" and determine your selling price.

Your Cost Sheet should look like this:

Plant Pot for "MONTH":

Color #1 _____   Color #2 _____ Color #3 _____

Pot cost =

Soil cost=

Plant #1 cost=

Plant #2 cost=

Plant #3 cost =

Top coat (Orchid Bark) =

Always water the posts after you make them up and give them a drink every 3 days.

If the Total Pot Costs $5.00, offer it for $10.00 for regular months and $15.00 for special months like Valentine's, 4th of July, Halloween and Christmas and you can also offer a special arrangement for a birthday. These pots can have an extra plant and a decorative "pick" like a heart, a flag, a ghost and something for Christmas. Look up Holiday Floral Picks online for ideas.

Be creative and always do your best to assure client satisfaction. Also offer to give a credit for your dried out pots being exchanged for new ones. Look at your cost sheet and see the cost of the pot and potting soil and make them a deal especially if they are willing to get a fresh pot every month and probably going to throw the dead pot anyway. You are recycling the supplies.

Now you are ready to **advertise**. Have Mom or Dad help design and print up a flyer. Take some to the neighbors especially the elderly who may not be able to work in the garden anymore. Also have Mom and Dad pass out flyers at work and tell grandparents, aunts and uncles too. The phone number you advertise with should be the **Google Voice Number**, never your private cell phone.

Advertise and schedule pots for delivery the 1st weekend of each month so you can accumulate orders and get a 50% down payment to cover supplies. Do not buy plants until it is time to assemble for delivery and try to have enough orders to use up all the fresh plants. Also buy flowering plants with buds that are just starting to open, using completely open flowers will not last long and clients will not be happy with their short life.

After all the pots are delivered and you have been paid calculate your cost and profit. Don't forget to pay expenses first, your transportation for supplies (this is an Indirect cost because you are using another person), then replace the cost of inventory (supplies) even if you will buy them next month, then bank the profit.

Something Special:

Curly Bamboo Arrangements are very popular for home or for a work area at the job. They are very hardy and since they are in water they require nothing else. There is only 1 Rule with Curly Bamboo - Never give Curly Bamboo any liquid fertilizer, it will kill them – they thrive on plain faucet water or bottled water if the client chooses. You don't need to change it just add more.

This is what you need for Curly Bamboo Arrangements:

- Curly Bamboo
- Interesting Bottles or Small Vases
- Silk Flower Spikes
- Decorative Cord of gold with red, green or black
- Colored Marbles

Curly Bamboo in a bottle with marbles and rocks

Buy Curly Bamboo in bulk in Chinatown or you Asian shopping area. Look for a shop that sells them in bulk bunches of short, medium and tall height bamboo. A bunch will always be your best **Price Point** for profit. If you're buying 1 or 2 pieces at a time you are already paying retail.

Interesting Bottles are usually empty liquor bottles. These may be hard to find but maybe Dad can help collect bottles for you from his friends and/or maybe from a local bar or restaurant. You want something tall, with a heavy base and an opening large enough for marbles to pass thru.

This is your most profitable design: This design will use one bamboo, one small to medium flower spike, some marbles and decorative cord.

If you can't find liquor bottles you can use small vases. This design will take 3 bamboos, a large, medium and small; a medium flower spike, enough pebbles or marbles to weight down the base and hold the bamboo securely and decorative cord.

Calculate the costs per item just as with the flower pots and sell each for minimum 2 to 2 ½ times the cost. Remember you will usually not replace these but will have the opportunity to sell them to others who see them and want one of their own.

Offer a flower spike with each arrangement to add color, match the flower color to the marble color if you can and decorate the vase or bottle with a couple of turn of cord and leave a "tail" or a 4 – 6 inch length of cord hanging down.

You can also offer Chinese symbols to hang on the cords. Your Asian supply shop may carry some or you can find them online. Many are for good luck, prosperity and love. Again get the cost plus tax and shipping and offer at 2 or 2 ½ times costs as an extra item.

志	美	仁	清	命	慈	華
ambition	beauty	benevelence	clarity	destiny	compassion	glory
恩	信	氣	明	永		恕
grace	devotion	energy	enlightenment	eternity		forgiveness
愛	福	實	和	貴		孝
love	happiness	honesty	harmony	honor		piety
誠	忠	孚	愁	忍	平	孚
sincerity	loyalty	meaning	melancholy	patience	peace	truth
洪	禮	示	協	義	聖	英
profundity	propriety	revelation	unity	righteousness	sage	courage
神	道	安	崇	健	德	智
spirit	the way	tranquility	reverence	vigor	virtue	wisdom

When you get paid - remember to replace the cost of supplies so you can make and sell more arrangements then Bank the Profit.

Financial Facts #2 - Rule of 72 Invented by Albert Einstein

Basically you divide the interest you are earning in your savings account by 72 to see how long it takes for **your money to double**. This is called simple interest.

Let's say at 29 you have $10,000.00 saved earning 4% annual interest.

72 divided by 4 = 18 or 18 years to get to $20,000.00:

- At 47 (29+18) you'll have $20,000.00
- At 65 (47+18) you'll have $40,000.00

Now let's change the interest to 12%, at 29 you have $10,000.00.

72 divided by 12 = 6 years to double your money.

- At 35 (29 +6) you'll have $20,000.00.
- At 41 (35+6) you'll have $40,000.00.

See the difference interest rate makes?

Go You Tube and see "The Million Dollar Baby IUL" to see how compound interest works. (www.youtube.com/watch?v=jXIPwCpANO0)

Now look at where your savings actually are, in your bank.

Let's be generous and say they are paying you 1% annual interest – it's actually less than 1 %. **72 divided by 1 = 72!**

That's right! At your bank, it will take 72 years for your money to double. So why save money at a bank?

If you have a credit card, auto loan or mortgage from that same bank what are you paying them in interest?

Understanding these Important Financial Concepts is mandatory in order to accumulate and access tax free wealth for later.

How much later is up to you and how much you have at different ages depends on how much you Pay Yourself First Every Week and where you are saving it and the interest you are being paid!

To see the variables of time and money and compounding interest, see pages 49 – 53.

Baking
If you like baking cakes then you'll love this opportunity.

This section will allow you to build a business offering your clients a one 8" layer cake or 6 jumbo size cupcakes (muffin size) or 12 regular size cupcakes using just 1 cake mix and with only basic frosting skills!

Everyone loves cake and the recipes I have included for you are my signature flavors that everyone loves and asks for. The recipes are for a Triple Chocolate Cake with buttercream frosting and for a Banana Sour Cream Cake with cream cheese frosting and they are very, very yummy.

As with any business you will need tools and inventory. Tools are reusable items and inventory is the supplies consumed with every order.

Tools for this business include:

- 1 Wilton 8 x 3 cake pan and Original Pam Cooking Spray
- 1 muffin pan for 6 muffins and muffin paper cups
- 1 cupcake pan for 12 cupcakes and paper cupcake cups
- 1 package of 12 inch round cake bases with foil
- A Lazy Susan helps to decorate easier
- A frosting knife
- A hand mixer
- A large bowl for mixing ingredients
- A large spoon for filling muffin and cupcake cups

- Wilton #17 decorating tip, a tip coupler and a package of frosting bags

Your inventory depends on the flavor you are making. **The ingredient list calls for specific brands of items, only use the brand specified for a Winning Result**. Winning Results equals satisfied clients and satisfied clients come back and buy again plus refer you to their family and friends. Also using the same ingredients every time equals consistency of taste and **clients like it to taste the same every time.**

Again you don't need any special frosting skills for now. If you start getting requests for some special design like flowers with leaves you can always use small silk flowers for now and look for a cake decorating class at your local Michaels or craft store later. Classes go from basic to advanced and you can really build exceptional skills with practice but for now its basic looks but yummy products. Try the recipes for yourself and your family. Here are the recipes and **DO NOT** use the instructions on the box **or substitute** any ingredient that says "only this brand".

#1 Triple Chocolate Cake:

Before mixing, set oven to 350 degrees and prepare your baking pan by spraying the bottom and edge generously with Original PAM. Don't worry if the cake sticks – frosting can fix anything.

- 1 package Duncan Hines Devil's Food Cake or Chocolate Fudge   (only this brand)
- 1 small box of JELLO Brand Chocolate Fudge or Chocolate Instant Pudding (only this brand)
- 4 large eggs
- ½ cup Crisco Vegetable Oil (only this brand and flavor)
- ¾ cup of water
- 1 cup regular (not diet or low fat) Sour Cream

Mix at medium speed just until blended – over mixing will cause a flat cake.

After blending ingredients with and mixer use a large spoon to add a 8oz package of Toll House Mini Chocolate Morsels, chocolate chips, (only this brand) to the mix.

The Minis stay mixed while the regular size goes to the bottom and can burn while baking and ruin your cake.

Fill your pan with all the mix and **bake** for 40 minutes. Note that all ovens bake differently when set to same temperature. The 8 x 3 cake takes 55 minutes in my oven. At 40 minutes **Test** your cake by pulling out the oven rack with the cake pan on it and insert a butter knife into the center. If it comes out with cake batter on it then your cake needs more time, test again in 10 minutes. Knife will come out completely clean when cake is cooked all the way thru.

When cake is done, turn cake upside down onto a cake round and cool, if cake sticks to pan, don't worry, frosting fixes everything and you'll learn to determine how much PAM to use in your pan. Cake must be completely cool to the touch, top and under the cake board, before you can frost so set it aside while you make the frosting or use the pan for another cake.

As you get busy with more orders you can cook 4 pans at a time in your oven as long as the pans don't touch each other or the sides of the oven. Touching will cause Hot Spots and burn the cake in that area and ruin it.

Buttercream Frosting:

Keep it Simple - Chocolate Cake & Chocolate Frosting

- 1 Crisco White Shortening Stick (1 = 1 cup, butter flavor is ok if just making chocolate frosting and not coloring frosting)
- 1 bag (2 pounds) Powdered Sugar

- ½ cup water
- 1 teaspoon salt- put in water and stir until salt dissolves
- 2 teaspoon regular (brown) vanilla *
- ½ cup Hershey's Cocoa Powder

if you plan to color this frosting then you will need to **only use white Crisco and white vanilla** by Wilton Cake Decorating Supplies. Brown vanilla and yellow Crisco will not allow your color to develop well.

Mix everything together until smooth.

If cake is cool, top and bottom, you're ready to frost.

Put cake on Lazy Susan and get your frosting knife and get a large scoop of frosting and start on top.

Only frost in 1 direction or you will fill your frosting with cake crumbs.

Frost with one hand in long strokes and turn the Lazy Susan slowly with the other hand. Level out the top of the frosting – even if the cake is crooked or broken. The goal is to have the top flat. Don't worry of the surface is rough, I'll give you a smoothing tip later.

Now frost the sides and be sure to fill in any spaces between the bottom of the cake and the cake board. Use the same technique – frost with one hand and move the Lazy Susan with the other. You should have enough frosting on the sides to cover the cake. Smooth out as best as possible and even out the edge between the sides and the top.

Now for a super sooth top and side- fill a tall coffee cup with very hot water. Wipe off your frosting knife and dip and hold it in the hot water for a few seconds. Then start at the top and lightly smooth out the surface from side to side. Clean off excess frosting and Dip your knife as often as need to keep smoothing.

Once you are happy with the top continue to the sides. Make the frosting as level as possible even if the cake is crooked. You will accumulate a little bit of water along the edge that you can clean up with a paper towel when done.

The Grand Finale-Clean off the water around the edge and prepare your frosting bag to decorate the edge of the top and the base.

If you're not comfortable decorating with frosting yet then you can do an edge with sprinkles. If you are using silk flowers ton top, match the sprinkles color to the flowers – ONLY use cake sprinkles to decorate. Everything should be edible except for the silk flowers. Be sure to rinse and dry and silk items you are putting on your cakes.

Cut off the tip edge of the frosting bag and put the coupler connecter inside, put your tip in the screw part of the connector and attach to the frosting bag. Fill the bag half way and start frosting around the top edge of the cake.

When done with the top, frost around the base. You will later learn how to use the **piped edge** (the design made by a frosting tip) as your cutting guide. Decorating is very easy to do but you will need practice.

You can keep leftover frosting and practice a couple of times a week without having a cake. Use a plastic placemat to do frosting edges on then scrap it off, refill your bag and start again. You will master the pressure required to create different patterns from the same tip. This #17 tip is my favorite and I use it on every cake that requires decorating. Later you can buy a #7 tip and practice writing with frosting.

#2 The Banana Sour Cream Cake

This cake **does not** require a decorated edge because the frosting is different. It **does require** some prior planning because it requires ripe bananas. You can also preplan your banana needs by buying them early then freezing when ripe. I like 3 large bananas or 4 small bananas per cake mix. Look at what size the market has then buy enough for 1 to 3 mixes. Ripen at home for a few more days then peel and freeze by cake mix need. This means if the bananas are large and you will use 3 per mix then freeze 3 together. This way you pull out a bag with only what you need for today's baking.

NOTE: If Mom or Dad has plants in the yard you can bury the banana peels and egg shells around them to feed them instead of throwing them away.

Here is the cake recipe:

- Bananas per mix
- ¼ cup sugar
- 1 teaspoon vanilla (brown- keep the white for colored frosting)
- 1 Duncan Hines Yellow or Butter Cake Mix (only this brand)
- 1 cup sour cream (regular not low fat or diet)
- 3 large eggs
- ¼ cup Crisco Vegetable Oil (only this brand and flavor)

Prepare your pan and turn on oven to 350 F.

Cream (blend) the defrosted bananas with any juice with the sugar and vanilla. When this is chunky add the rest of the ingredients.

Blend ingredients until moistened – remember overmixing causes a flat cake.

Bake for 40 minutes then test every 10 minutes until knife comes out clean.

Turn out onto your cake round to cool. Remember, frosting fixes everything so don't worry if cake sticks.

Here is the frosting recipe: Remember to frost the cake only when it's completely cool.

- 1 package 8 oz. Philadelphia Cream Cheese*
- 1 16 oz. Package Powdered Sugar

Cream the cheese and add the sugar, in 3 parts and mix. Add a little water for smoothness, if needed. Set aside ¼ cup water and add by **one** teaspoon at a time then mix. Frost in one direction, as with chocolate cake, then you can lightly do a back and forth pattern on top if not decorating with silk flowers.

DO NOT use the hot water to smooth out this frosting, it will melt the cream cheese and your frosting will not stay put.

Cost your ingredients on either cake then increase 2 -3x to get your selling price. You can round up to nearest dollar for an even amount. Suggest you bake and decorate each 1x then advertise with flyers and get going.

Keep your tools clean and check stock after every job and replace cake rounds and frosting bags so you don't run out. Use a calendar to record your orders and have the baked goods picked up or delivered the next day. I suggest you bake on Friday for a Saturday pick up or bake on Sunday for Mom & Dad to deliver to work on Monday.

Replace your inventory to be ready for next week's orders. **Get 50% down** in cash when you take your order and the **balance in cash when you deliver** and **give a receipt** with your **Google Voice Number** for reorders and include a new baking flyer with every delivery.

Allocate funds to inventory and more tools if needed and pay a small kitchen use fund to Mom then Bank the Rest in your envelopes according to your formula.

Our Mission Statement

The Life Goal of The Wise Woman's Academy is to teach every Teen, regardless of age, Chief Financial Officer Skills to be able to Self Determine their personal financial security.

We deal with money every day, year in and year out but are never taught how to optimize money.

We are not taught finance or even budgeting during our basic education process and any college finance classes we may experience are usually related to business money management and not personal money management and maximization.

Our C.F.O. (Chief Financial Officer) Training Manuals are designed for the different stages of life and will teach all you need to know about making your money work for you and having everything you dream of having sooner instead of later or never.

Painting & Bling Work

Painting and Bling Work are creative projects and can be very lucrative, meaning they can make you a lot of money, consistent money.   For our purposes painting will be learning to paint holiday tee shirts using Tri–Chem Paints and Instructions by a long time Tri-Chem Teacher. We like their paints because they last forever on fabrics and the skills you learn will be from easy and fast to very advanced and you can easily progress   from painting tee shirts to doing paintings and anything else fabric.

 Plus the Teacher has offered to put together Holiday Kits of paints and a DVD so you can create and sell tee shirts for Holiday months. We will also have the DVD on our website in the Girl's Support section for you to review and study.

Just think a moment, how many holidays are in the year? Not sure? Then flip thru a calendar – there are a lot. Ask any woman and I'm sure she'll say she has several holiday shirts and would be interested in more shirts. Cha-Ching – you can supply those holiday shirts. You can also supply more items as your skills grow, as long as an item is fabric, you can paint it.

Again, the kits come with the colors you'll need for that month's holiday designs and a DVD you keep for training and to build your visual Painting Library. You can order the Holiday Kits with Paints and DVDs from patmayfield@juno.com.

For this Mini-Business you will need **a Dedicated Workspace**, a table in your room is best so you can leave your work laid out to dry. You can start with a card table then expand to a 6 foot x 18 or x30 wide table as your business and projects grow and depending on the available space in your room. You will also need some organizing storage drawers that will allow you to keep your supplies and colors put away when not in use. This keeps your work space clean and organized and allows you find what you are looking for easily. You can also add stick on labels on the drawers that itemize what is inside.

You can also make this business easier by having your clients supply the tee shirt or sweat shirt they want you to paint a design on then you just charge them for **material and labor**. Also work up a couple of sample tee shirts for advertising for Mom and Dad to show at work and one for you to wear so your friends and class mates and see and order from you. Also take a picture and make a catalog album of all your work to show clients.

If you are willing to start painting but not with designs from scratch then you may want to do just a **"Bling Work Business" with glittering and/or beadwork** on existing garments with designs. You can **Bling Out** anything by outlining a figure, an abstract or text with liquid glitter paint by Tri-Chem or by sewing on different colors and sizes of beads around the design. You can do this on baseball style hats, baby clothes and many other things. You are only limited by your imagination.

Tools:
- Workspace and drawers for supplies
- Tee shirt board

Inventory:
- Holiday designs and paint tube kits
- Glitter paint tubes
- Beads, needles and thread
- Tee shirts for your samples

Practice **Bling Out** on a few of Mom's older shirts and a couple of baseball hats just to get ideas and a feel for this type of crafting.

I suggest you plan ahead and work up samples to start showing 2 weeks **before the holiday month**, this means have Valentine's Day sample shirts ready to show in the middle of January. Also make flyers and advertise your Holiday Designs and your Bling Out Service on the same flyer so clients can start getting ideas and think about the things in their closet that need some Bling.

You can take a picture of your flyer and text or email it to me, if you like, for checking.

As you painting skills grow you will learn to use stencils and iron on transfers to expand and your designs. You can do more complicated projects and bigger items like table cloths and pictures if you like. You can also paint a lot of small things like monograms or small designs on baby and children's clothes.

As with any business, you are only limited by your imagination.

Financial Facts #3 - Something to Think About

Where do you Dream to be financially in 5, 10 or 20 years? Want your own business. Great, but you need funds.

This is what it takes to have a Million Dollars, Tax Free at 65 or sooner.

Learn to Pay Yourself First and Allow Funds to Mature to fund you Dream.

This is how compounding interest uses time to grow money.

See "The Million Dollar Baby IUL" Video on YouTube for a crash course on compounding interest.

BUILDING A MILLION-DOLLAR RETIREMENT ACCOUNT
Daily or monthly investments suggested to build $1,000,000 by age 65.

STARTING AGE	DAILY SAVINGS	MONTHLY SAVINGS	YEARLY SAVINGS
20	$2.00	$61	$730
25	$3.57	$109	$1,304
30	$6.35	$193	$2,317
35	$11.35	$345	$4,144
40	$20.55	$625	$7,500
45	$38.02	$1,157	$13,879
50	$73.49	$2,235	$26,824
55	$156.12	$4,749	$56,984

Cell Phone Photography

This is possibly the easiest "Business" you could do because you already have the most expensive component –your cell phone- and have access to everything else you need on line thru Apps on your phone.

You already have a camera and photo edit app installed on your phone and they are very easy to use. You can also print pictures on any of the online services available. We like and use Snapfish.com which gives you 100 free 4x6 pictures a month for the first year and offers everything you want or need to put photos on too.

Tools:

- Your cell phone and your brain

Inventory:

- None

Advertise your Photo Service to include:

Taking Pictures of toddlers, kids or pets

Taking pictures of pictures for editing and enlargements. Many people have a **single picture** that they love but it's small. By taking a picture of a picture you can enhance it then enlarge it, put it on a canvas, a shirt or a cup to bring Happiness to that individual.

Photo color correction, color edit or content correction - Many camera photos fade with time especially if exposed in a frame or have excess space in the picture that can be taken out. Your service can correct these issues.

Collages from a Family Event – you can take pictures of their pictures and make a collage or photobook for a client.

Custom Theme Work - Your client may want a collage of all their children's wedding pictures on the same enlargement or a collage of a parent or grandparent while growing up.

You can do any type of custom work from your client's box of photographs especially if they are older and have no technology skills.

Again your Offerings are limited by your imagination.

Advertising – again design a flyer detailing the above services with your **Google Voice Number** AND for this business I also suggest Business Cards.

Pet Pictures are BIG BUSINESS but where can you take your pet to get a good photo? Go to your local Dog Park with or without a simple costume, maybe a hat and neck scarf, and take pictures of the pet and the pet and owner. Important take a tablet and have the owner write in big letters his or her name, phone number and the pets name and take a photo of them holding up the tablet. Tell them you will not call to bug them but only send a reminder text. Note: never text any photos because you have now given away your product – however you can text them the image of any picture they buy along with the printed copy or copies.

Give them your card and ask how long they will be there so you have time to edit the pics.

Photograph about 2 or 3 dogs and owners then sit and edit. Do your homework and have the cost of sizes and a possible packet price and content already set up. Show the owners the pics they can order.

If they order now – have a receipt book and detail what they want – which pics in which sizes and get a mailing address on their photo info page.

Set up a **PayPal Account to collect a payment** with a debit or credit card with your phone. Many people like Pay Pal because the vendor – YOU - does not keep any personal information on the person or their credit or debit card info.

If they want to think about it- tell them you will save the pics for 2 weeks. Double check their contact info on your tablet and make sure they have your card. Text them one time only next week to remind them that you are saving their pictures and again, one time only the following week – you don't want to be a pest! NOTE: you can also download all your pictures to Snapfish.com and save them in album forever.

They may not buy these pictures but may call you for a future picture – **remember there are not a lot of places to get a good pet photo.** Schedule them to come to you at home when an adult is present and that there is a $5.00 sitting fee payable in cash upon arrival. Have a work space set up and an adult present with you at all times. Have a fee schedule already printed up when they arrive with some individual, packets and product prices. Remember, these you will buy from Snapfish.com so **mark up** or increase their prices to cover your profit. Maybe use a corner of the garage with a gray backdrop, this is a good neutral shade. Also begin to collect costumes for boy dogs and girl dogs just to make the photos have more personality. Again you will edit the photos while they are there and have prices and packets ready for them. Have them pick and pay on you PayPal app and don't forget their mailing address for mailing or they can arrange to come by and pick up their order when mom or dad is home.

Again this business is only limited by your imagination and can lead to a **Super Profitable LIFE LONG Part Time Business** doing event photography for babies, birthdays, parties and even weddings with your phone or a tablet and also being able to offer a large variety of products with the pictures you have taken.

You decide how you will make money to fund your lifestyle.

Business Needs:

1. Decide which Home Based Business you will work & Develop a 12 month Business Plan in writing and review your progress every month.

2. Create a Google Voice Number to use for your Mini Business on advertising flyers which rings on your cell phone. When this number is dialed it shows up as your caller ID number so you know it's a business call and not a social call so you can answer professionally. You will also be able to dial out, return client calls, on this Google number so you can keep your personal number private.

3. Mom or Dad can set up a checking account for you at Chase. The account is called Chase High School Checking for 13-17 year olds. It comes with your personal ATM card and will allow you to access funds for business needs and set up transfer of excess funds* to your IUL Cash Account to earn 8-12% annual interest and builds your income stream for later in life when account is matures.

4. Set up a Pay Pal Account that deposits into your checking account. Remember clients like using Pay Pal.

5. Have Mom or Dad set up an IUL for themselves and one for you. This "Savings Account" is an Insurance Product with a face value and also a Cash Accumulation Account (a Future Income Stream). This IUL will require mom or you to deposit a monthly premium and also allow you to double the premium* with a deposit to the Cash Account to grow your future income stream. Watch the Million Dollar Baby IUL on You Tube again to understand why saving in an IUL give you all the benefits and no losses.

6. Remember an IUL pays annual interest of 8-12% with no losses and allows you to access funds Tax Free after maturity. Study the charts on pages 49 – 51 to see why saving this way in your Teens becomes a Huge Advantage when you're 35.

7. Have Questions or need help finding an IUL Agent? Email me at jjnoccoauthor@gmail.com for a referral.

Saving and Growing Funds

STUDY THIS SECTION VERY WELL &

SHARE THIS SECTION with MOM & DAD

When we started our training, we were working with limited income from our weekly allowance. Now by building your Mini-Business you may now have access to a larger amount of money on a weekly basis. So does this mean you can spend more every week? **NO** – you are still going to follow some of the same principles you have already learned and learn some new financial facts. As you saw, some of the mini –businesses deal with perspiration and others with inspiration and creativity. So you choose what works for you.

In Financial Facts #1 you saw how money grows in a Fixed Account, a Variable Account and in an Indexed Account. Here we will go into more detail on the Best Option to Grow Funds without any Risk or Losses. Just to review:

A Fixed Account like a bank checking account or savings account accumulates your money but pays you less than 1% interest. This means that your money will take 72 years to double. Review Financial Fact #4 on page 29.

A Variable Account is any "Qualified Account" like a 401K account can grow your money but it usually loses money because of the way the plan is structured. A Variable Account is tied to the Stock Market so when stocks go up – you make money but when the stocks go down you lose money. Your balance is never the same and you cannot depend on having a certain amount of money at a certain point in time. These types of accounts usually adjust or lose money every 7 financial years, which is crazy because they are advertised to be safe money maximizing or retirement funding accounts. Also these types of accounts are Tax Deferred Accounts meaning you pay taxes later – **Very Scary** -

47

you know what todays tax rate is but the future rate is unknown so why risk losing a higher percent of your money than you need to when you worked very hard to save it and are older?

Study this table to understand how Qualified 401k Plans have performed from 1998 to 2012 and see how an **IUL's Floor** makes a difference in your balance. Also keep in mind this type of account adjusts about every 7 years and not to your favor.

Comparison of Historical Performance of
S & P 500 Index and IUL

	401k/IRA		Index Universal Life	
S & P	Point to Point	$100,000	IUL 0-12%	$100,000
1998	26.06%	126,060	12.00%	112,000
1999	18.76%	149,709	12.00%	125,440
2000	-12.13%	131,549	0.00%	125,440
2001	-8.87%	119,881	0.00%	125,440
2002	-24.67%	90,306	0.00%	125,440
2003	24.26%	112,214	12.00%	140,493
2004	8.90%	122,202	8.90%	152,997
2005	4.86%	128,141	4.86%	160,432
2006	11.20%	142,492	11.20%	178,401
2007	4.09%	148,320	4.09%	185.697
2008	-43.98%	83,089	0.00%	185,697
2009	24.89%	103,770	12.00%	207,981
2010	14.07%	118,370	12.00%	232,939
2011	2.69%	121,554	2.69%	239,205
2012	11.63%	135,691	11.63%	267,024
After Tax	est 30%	$95,000	Tax Free	$267,024

An Indexed Universal Account is the Best Way to Save and Grow Funds at a High Interest rate with **NO RISK & NO LOSSES**. This type of Cash Accumulation Account is structured completely different from the Qualified Accounts, but is not commonly well-known because it is tied to a Life Insurance Product and managed by the Life Insurance Companies. The structural points that make it different from a Fixed Account and a Variable Account are as follows:

NO RISK & NO LOSSES means that you never lose your deposits into this account because it has a structured **"FLOOR"** meaning that if the stocks attached to this account lose money you never lose your money it just stays the same. See the Indexed Universal Life Account during the years 2000-2003 on the previous page.

The Life Insurance Policy containing this account has 2 parts, the life insurance part and the high cash accumulation part that **you can deposit excess funds** into to earn up to 15%+ interest, the average annual growth is 8-12%. This is **ENORMOUS INTEREST** compared to less than 1% at the Bank. The 15% is called the **CAP** meaning that this is the maximum amount the insurance company will pay you even if interest goes up to 25% or more. After all this is fair, getting interest up to 15% is reasonable considering they take care of our money and manage all the accounting needed to make sure we have our money when we need it and our family gets paid when it comes time to collect on the policy.

So again, an Indexed Universal Life Account has a **"FLOOR"** that keeps us from losing our money and a **"CAP"** that allows up to make up to 15% **With Out any RISK or TAXES**.

Yes, Life Insurance Policies receive favorable treatment from the IRS meaning that any Policy Face Money paid to a family and the Excess of any cash in the Cash Accumulation Policy in the life insurance policy is paid TAX FREE to the recipient or beneficiary.

Having an IUL Account inside of a Life Insurance Policy has only 1 Rule – you must qualify in terms of health.

Saving and Growing Excess Funds

To some people, Millennial means being born in a certain year or being of a particular age. However, in The Wise Woman's World, "Millennial" means being able to develop your favorite interest into a business that can help fund the lifestyle that you want to live – sooner rather than later or never.

Wait – didn't we already do this? Yes, you already are or have structured your Mini-Business and are beginning to see success and are saving the profits IN YOUR Chase account to deposit into your IUL so let's move on. For more info see Volume 4 The Wise Teen's Guide to Building Your Millennial Life with E-Commerce.

Here are the Steps to Building Your Millennial Life:

1- See the "Million Dollar Baby IUL Video" on You Tube to understand how compound interest works.

2- Have Mom contact me to discuss setting up an IUL for her and set one up for you too and finding a local agent. You only want to set up an IUL Insurance Policy **NEVER** a Term Life Policy. See page 46 for info on "Term Policy" vs "IUL Policy".

3- Deposit your excess funds monthly into Your High Interest Cash Accumulation Account inside Your IUL to Build your Personal Bank and mature the funds over time.

4- Review the table "How to Have a Million at 65" on the next page and note that the table begins at age 20 and saves $2.00 a day for 45 years. Also review the "Miss Save Early" Table and the "Miss Wait Longer" Tables on the next 2 pages and note that they begin at age 25.

You are starting this No Risk High Interest Money Maximizing Plan up to _5-10 years sooner_ than those tables and will have _Financial Options_ earlier in your life than at age 48 or 65!

STARTING AGE	DAILY SAVINGS	MONTHLY SAVINGS	YEARLY SAVINGS
20	$2.00	$61	$730
25	$3.57	$109	$1,304
30	$6.35	$193	$2,317
35	$11.35	$345	$4,144
40	$20.55	$625	$7,500
45	$38.02	$1,157	$13,879
50	$73.49	$2,235	$26,824
55	$156.12	$4,749	$56,984

Saving $2.00 a day at 20 years old is very easy but you have to wait till 65 to draw the income stream.

This is a Better Option:

By using your Mini-Business to earn an extra $10.00 or more a day and depositing that into your IUL Cash Account you build a bigger dollar amount in half the time to draw as a Tax Free Income Stream in your 30's or 40's.

MISS SAVE EARLY

This Table shows what saving $10.00 a Day can grow into in 17 years. Note that the Total Contributions are for 7 years and **start at age 25**. IUL's are "customizable" and can be paid a certain length of time then allowed to mature for 17 years with 8-12% compound interest.

This table shows 8% interest.

Also an IUL will have a regular monthly contribution amount but you can Double Pay that amount monthly to have your money work for you faster to increase the cash accumulation account growing at High Interest. Your Mini-Business and Your IUL allow you to start maximizing your funds at an earlier age like 15 and double deposit for 7 years. Review the "Million Dollar Baby IUL' on YouTube again to better understand compound interest with No Loses or Risk and the options having your own Bank gives you.

AGE	YEARLY CONTRIBUTIONS	TOTAL ACCUMULATION
25	$3,600.00	$ 3,888.00
26	$3,600.00	$ 8,087.00
27	$3,600.00	$ 12,622.00
28	$3,600.00	$ 17,520.00
29	$3,600.00	$ 22,809.00
30	$3,600.00	$ 28,522.00
31	$3,600.00	$ 34,692.00
32	$0	$ 37,467.00

33	$0	$ 40,467.00
34	$0	$ 43,702.00
35	$0	$ 47,198.00
36	$0	$ 50,974.00
37	$0	$ 55,052.00
38	$0	$ 59,456.00
39	$0	$ 64,212.00
40	$0	$ 69,349.00
41	$0	$ 74,897.00
42	$0	$ 80,889.00
43	$0	$ 87,360.00
44	$0	$ 94,349.00
45	$0	$ 101,897.00
46	$0	$ 110,048.00
47	$0	$ 118,852.00
48	$0	$ 128,361.00

TOTAL CONTRIBUTION $25,200.00 FOR 7 YEARS

OR UP TO $50,400.00 IF DOUBLE DEPOSITING

WILL BE ABOUT $256,722.00+ AT 48 YEARS OLD!

THIS IS THE GAME PLAN YOU WANT TO MAXIMIZE.

MISS WAIT LONGER

In this Table saving $10.00 a day did not **start until age 32**.

You may look at the "Bottom Line" and think that the TOTALS are not that different, $128,361.00 and $131,221.00. However, the Contribution Total of $61,200.00 is 2 X plus the $25,200.00.

The time contributions from the *Miss Early Table* is 7 years and 17 for   the *Miss Later Table*. This is how Time & Compound Interest Work.
Look at *Table Early* and find where your $25,200.00 Doubles.

Table Early Doubles to $50,974.00 at 36.
Table Later Doubles from $61,200.00 to $117,901.00 at 47.

Having Financial Options at 46 is Good but Having Financial Options at 36 is GREAT!

AGE ACCUMULATION	YEARLY CONTRIBUTION	TOTAL
25	$0	$-
26	$0	$-
27	$0	$-
28	$0	$-
29	$0	$-
30	$0	$-
31	$0	$-

32	$3,600.00	$3,888.00
33	$3,600.00	$8,087.00
34	$3,600.00	$12,622.00
35	$3,600.00	$17,520.00
36	$3,600.00	$22,809.00
37	$3,600.00	$28,533.00
38	$3,600.00	$34,692.00
39	$3,600.00	$41,355.00
40	$3,600.00	$48,552.00
41	$3,600.00	$56,324.00
42	$3,600.00	$64,718.00
43	$3,600.00	$73,783.00
44	$3,600.00	$83,574.00
45	$3,600.00	$94,148.00
46	$3,600.00	$105,567.00
47	$3,600.00	$117,901.00
48	$3,600.00	$131,221.00

TOTAL CONTRIBUTION $61,200.00 FOR 17 YEARS

Study this Carefully

In the *How to have a Million Dollars at 65 Table* **a 20 year old saves $2.00 a Day for 45 years** – Too Little Money for Too Long a Time! Saving $61 a month for 12 months is $730 a year for 45 Years is $32,400.00 in Total Contributions. The interest rate is undisclosed in this table but it is a compounding interest account. This is OK if you are doing nothing else in those 45 years except working a 9-5. **Most Individuals are ready for Financial Options around 35-40**. With this plan, You have few Financial Options to Having and Living your Millennial Life.

In the *Miss Save Early Table* **a 25 year old saves $10.00 a day for 7 years** or $300.00 a month for 12 months is $3,600.00 and is $25,200.00 in Total Contributions. At 8% compounding interest the $25,200.00 in contributions are double just 5 years after you **stop paying** at the age of 36.

THINK ABOUT THIS: **a 15 year old saves $10.00 a day (about $50.00 a week) for 7 years** you stop contributions at 22. Plan on allowing your money to mature and grow for 10 years or more. Your contributions are the same $25,200.00 however by starting 10 years younger at 15 not 25, now your contributions are double at 27. **At 27 you may be married and have your first child and now have an alternate income stream to stay at home till your child starts school a 4 or 5.** Also note that with your Home Based Business you can *double the contributions* to $20.00 a day. This will double your contributions to $50,400.00 for 7 years but also give you a Larger Tax Free Income Stream that you can draw on in the years when money is tight because you are raising children. Or you may want to see the world for 12 month before settling down. Or you may need funds to expand your Mini-Business into a Full Grown Business and can borrow from your Personal Bank without qualifying for credit and repay if you choose. **Plan now to give yourself financial options in 15 - 20 years.**

YES, with discipline and planning here you can have Tax Free Financial Options!

In the _Miss Save Later Table_ **a 32 year old saves $10.00 a day for "17 years"** and stops contributions at 48 with a Total Contribution of $61,200.00. This contribution total doubles at 47 if no funds were drawn out in earlier years. The older we are the less patience we have to let money just sit and grow. There is always an emergency of some kind requiring money.

THINK ABOUT THIS: _The Miss Save Later Table_ is a common occurrence for your Mom's generation because of 2 very important financial facts. First, you are the first generation learning these Financial Facts before the age of 40.

Second, most women only become concerned with life insurance products at around 40 and usually never learn about how an IUL inside of a Life Insurance Policy can Maximize Money via compound interest. You are learning both of these facts at about 15 years old.

If you looked at the pages covering our Business Opportunity you will have noticed that the Wise Woman's Academy not only "Teaches Finance" but also "Works Finance". All of our Members are Life and Health Licensed in their states show clients the advantages of an IUL Policy over all other life insurance products because we believe this is the wisest and safest type of insurance investment that an individual can make without exception.

There are other Insurance/Investment Entities out there that promote the **"Buy Term and Invest the Rest"** type of thinking. Let me explain a few facts about this that are a Great Financial Disadvantage and Giant Client Disservice.

1. **Term Insurance** only offers to pay a face amount if the insured dies during the term of coverage. After the term is finished the insured has nothing. The policy can be $2.00, $5.00 or $20.00 a day but you have no cash accumulation

with this type of policy therefore only the life insurance company gets rich.

2. **Term Insurance is Temporary Insurance** and only good for a certain period of time. **An IUL is Permanent Insurance** and covers you for life or until age 100. The Face or amount of the Insurance payout may change if you stop contributing before the agreed upon date but will not change if you set up a pay 7 or pay 10 policy. The cash account will continue to grow until you begin to draw it.

3. **At the end of a Term Policy the Insured Needs to Health Qualify for a new policy.** If the insured developed a chronic illness or was in an accident which compromises his health and longevity he will not receive a new term policy and may not qualify for an IUL either. Also a new policy will cost double the monthly premium of the last policy because the insured is older. An IUL premium always stays the same but you can deposit more to the cash account.

4. **An IUL Policy is Good for Life.** Some Parents think its Bad Luck to insure a child but juvenile policies can grow in value as with the "Million Dollar Baby IUL" with a child PLUS Guarantee Insurability later in life regardless of health. Statistics show that babies thru 30 have a higher risk of accidental injury or illness that will make them uninsurable later in life. Again Mom contact me with any IUL questions or to find a local agent.

ATTENTION MOM:

Start with Today – Why Change?

Most people strongly dislike their job and are not making the income to live their IDEAL LIFE.

With this Strategic Planning Tool your Teen now has the Power to Dream, Plan and put into Action changes that will give them Freedom.

Freedom to Love what they do daily and the Freedom to earn what they want in less time so they have more time to do all the important things they want for them self and their family.

Money isn't Everything, but having Sufficient Spending Money on a daily, weekly, monthly basis makes Everything Else Easier.

Encourage your Teen to start Building Financial Freedom Today and build skills with their Home Based Business.

If none of the current suggestions are attractive, then what would your teen love to be doing daily for their income? Take a look at Volume 3 – Building your Millennial Life with E-Commerce.

Now let's look at you, How much do you take home weekly, after taxes? How much would you like to be taking home weekly? How are you going to accomplish this?

Going from here to there takes planning, goals and activities. If you have none of these plans in place now then they are on the path to having the same life and earning the same money for the next 50 years!

Think About Changes and get started working thru the exercises in this training manual to change your thinking and manifest your Ideal Life.

Financial Facts # 4-Your D. I. M. E. & Your Income

Let's work up your D. I. M. E. to see your "NOW" in black & white:

D = DEBT list all payments you are making (add lines if needed)

Auto Loan __monthly x 12=_____

Student Loan __monthly x 12=_____

Credit Cards ____monthly x 12=_____

I = INCOME list income from all sources

       Primary Income _monthly x 12=_____

       Secondary Income _monthly x 12=_____

M = Mortgage or Rent

_____monthly x12=_____

E = Expenses & Emergency Fund

Average Monthly Utilities & Cell Bills _x 12=_____

Average Monthly Food & Entertainment __x12=_____

Children's Monthly Expenses _x12=_____

Average Monthly Auto Expenses _x12=_____

Monthly Retirement Contributions _x12=_____

Emergency Savings Contributions __x12=_____

ANNUAL TOTAL IN_____ **TOTAL OUT**_____

BALANCE DISCRETIONARY FUNDS _____

The 401K Is <u>NOT</u> Your Friend

The 401K program was developed to shift the burden of managing and growing pensions from employers and moving the responsibility to a 3rd party.

Who are the biggest employers?

The government, the states and the cities are the largest national employers.

That's why the government got Wall Street involved in structuring a plan. Wall Street only cares about one thing, Commissions and Fees, money you pay them regardless if you, the individual investor, is winning or loosening.

Wall Street is the Master of Painting a Pretty Picture regardless of what actually happens.

After all Wall Street can blame the economy, the Fed or World Economic Conditions as a reason why you made no profits.

Need more proof?

Read the **Pirates of Manhattan** I & II by Barry J. Dyke and study the Historical Comparison of actual 401 vs IUL below.

Also note that drawing funds or borrowing from a 401k before 59 ½ has unfavorable conditions; 10% penalty, funds are added to current year's income and any funds drawn before 59 ½ must be paid back to the fund.

An IUL has none of these unfavorable conditions; funds can be drawn Tax Free at any age and you can pay back funds if you choose. However, funds should be mature for maximum yield to you.

Obstacles in Your Path: People – Time – Money

Roadblocks to change, yes, we all have them, however, most are related to time and money.

Learning to use our time productively to accomplish positive changes in our lives takes planning and perseverance.

Congratulations, this is exactly what you are learning with this training manual. You are clarifying what you want, why you want it and are planning and taking the steps needed to attain it.

Money or rather lack of sufficient money to cover everything we need or want is usually our biggest obstacle. Where you are today with your income and where you want to be is always on our mind.

Most people change jobs for 5 to 10 thousand more a year.

This is only $100 tom $200 more a week, less taxes, so it really doesn't produce much benefit or life style change but adds new stress and uncertainty.

So what does it take for you to produce the big bucks and have the ability to have more free time?

- Going Back to College for an uncertain job & racking up debt?
- Going to a Vocational School for an uncertain job & racking up debt?
- Playing the Lotto and hoping to win?
- Marry a Millionaire?

So What can You Really Do?

Introducing a Possible Option:
The Wise Woman's Academy Business Opportunity:

Mini in Terms of Cost - NOT in Terms of the Earnings Possible or the Business Entity You can Build

The Wise Woman's Academy offers a career path in Financial Services and Planning available in every US state. After licensing as a Life & Health Insurance Agent in your state, our Intensive Training System gives you World Class, Relevant Training that allows you to earn an extra $100.00 to $1000.00 a week or more by placing just 1 G.I.U.L (Guaranteed Indexed Universal Life) Insurance Policy a week on a part time basis – part time in hours required, approximately 4 to 6 per client, with better than full time pay (commission earned). The Goal is to Educate & Protect Families.

A G.I.U.L. is Superior to a 401K with No Risk and No Losses., see page 106. G.I.U.L insurance policy has proven it's historical worth with names such as Walt Disney of Disneyland, Max and Verda Foster of Foster Farms and Roy Kroc of McDonalds. These individuals and millions more have used money from their G.I.U.L. insurance policies to fund their dreams, Not just any insurance policy but a policy that includes an insurance policy face value as well as a high cash accumulation account.

The company we umbrella under is over 100 years old and in the Top1% of 8,000 Insurance Firms in the US. Some of their best features include the ability to offer products from many providers and almost always receive 100% commission in a 2 part 40-60 split rather in a 1/12 payment for 12 months as with an ordinary insurance company earnings agreements.. We include our online training University and webinars as well as are available as Mentors to you in personal one on one interaction via phone, video chat or Skype. We can also connect you to a weekly training group if you prefer that weekly meeting format.

63

Best of All, you are authorized to use any Wise Woman's Academy Publications to build your Business.

Like   what   you   see?
Step #1 is only $100.00 to enroll with us (CONTACT VIA EMAIL).

Step #2 is Life & Health training and licensing in your state.

Why a Career in Financial Planning

A career in Financial Planning gives you a Super Beneficial role in life. You are now able to easily and effectively fund the transition from your actual life to your Ideal Life starting part-time. With Us, You will Grow and Bloom where you are Planted – in your local area.

You will work inside a Success Module that will make your job easier by using the Wise Woman's Academy On-Line University for training around your schedule and will be authorized to use our Training Manuals as marketing tools for your business. You will network with other women in clubs and events locally. Have it your way - work alone at your own pace or build a team.

You will Do Good in the World and Love what you do – educate and help others protect their families and reach their financial goals in a risk free and timely manner. You will be able to put others on the path to their Ideal Lives by sharing what you have learned and using the tools you have at your fingertips.

In addition to helping others, you will transform yourself into the Master of Your Own Financial Destiny. The Wise Woman's Academy includes plans to expand and offers other Risk Free Venues to help you become the person you see in your Mind's Eye – that Successful Wonderful Person that can benefit, influence, and guide teens and adults to success in their personal lives and influence circles.

Financial Planning Opportunity

With Wise Women	With Other Companies
Income $120,000/yr +	Income $80,000/yr
Rep 30+ Companies	Rep 1 Company
Life & Health License 65+	Life & Health, Series 6 &
Advanced Commissions	No Advanced Commissions
No Quotas	Required Monthly Quotas
Hot Market	Cold Market
Serve 95% Population	Serve 5% Population
No Experience Needed	Need Tons of Experience
No Advertising Needed	Need Lots of Advertising
Master Tax Fee Strategies	Find & Build New Clients
Move $ via Risk Free Rollovers	Sell High Risk Securities
Explode Career & Income:	Limited Career & Income

Master Your Financial Planning Career, Build a Team, Earn Residual Income Streams & Build Your Financial Legacy

With The Wise Woman's Academy,

You're at the Right Place at the Right Time!

For detailed career-planning steps, email

jjnoccoauthor@gmail.com

Learning Objectives:

Page 8

1) What is an "instant gratification society" and where do we learn this?

2) On average, at what age do young adults ruin their credit?

3) Why will YOU not have this problem?

Page 10

4) Budgeting also teaches _____ _____.

Page 14

5) What are the 3 Wise Teen's Banking Rules?

6) Why choose something you like to build into a Mini-Business?

Page 16

7) Why advertise your Mini-Business with a flyer and what information should be included on it?

Page 18

8) What are inventory supplies?

9) Why is it important to cost your job?

Page 19

10) What is a variance?

11) What is the cost accounting formula?

Page 21

12) What is diversification?

Page 22

13) What is a Fixed Account?

14) What is a Variable Account?

15) What is an IUL or GIUL Account and why is this the Best Account to save money in?

Page 29

16) What is the Rule of 72 and why is it important for maximizing your savings?

17) How much annual interest does your bank pay and using the Rule of 72, how long will it take to double your money?

Page 37

18) What does the first line of our Mission Statement mean to you?

Page 41

19) Watch the "Million Dollar Baby IUL" on You Tube and explain compounding interest.

32) What is the advantage of starting to plan your Millennial Life while a teen?

Page 52/55

33) Who is smarter, Miss Save Early or Miss Wait Longer and why?

Page 58

34) What is the difference between an IUL Policy and a Term Life Policy?

35) Does a Term Life Policy have a Fixed Premium and a Cash Accumulation account?

Page 61

36) What is the penalty and pay back difference between a 401k Policy and an IUL Policy?

The *Wise Woman's* Academy®
Financial Training for Life

Six Volume Series:

- Be True to You – Success Training Manual
- The Wise Teens's Guide to Financial Facts & Entrepreneurial Basics
- The Wise Woman's Guide to Building Your Millennial Life with e-Commerce
- Wise Bride, Wise Mommy, Wise Divorcee
- The Wise Businesswoman, Funding the Next Step
- The Wise Woman's Guide to Retirement Planning & Structuring Inheritance

Join the
The *Wise Woman's* Academy®
and remember:
never put the keys to
your financial success
in someone else's
pocket.

Preview to the C F O Training

Be True to You - Success Training Manual

Ready to make the next 12 months pivotal to your success?

Success is a series of steps leading to accomplishments.

With this Exceptional Tool you'll learn to think outside the box to clarify, act and accomplish the goals and results you desire.

The Secret to our "Be True to You Success Training Manual" is dividing the 52 week year into 4 shorter, 12 week periods where you will be accountable to yourself and fast track your success.

You will focus on defining what you want and why you want it and record it in the book.

Then you will determine what activities are needed and where these will take place to assure your progress.

You are creating a contract with the person in charge – YOU.

This system puts you in the driver's seat by mapping out all the steps needed and building the big picture, laid out before your very own eyes, that leads to your Millennial Life.

Remember, a millennial builds skills and a system to support their lifestyle.

You will be 100% accountable to yourself by journaling weekly and evaluating your progress every 6 weeks to assure you're on track for your desired results.

Congratulations on allowing the Wise Woman's Academy to guide you on the path to your Best Self & Ideal Life.

Preview to the C F O Training

The Wise Teen's Guide
To Financial Facts & Entrepreneurial Basics

Learn to manage what you earn and how to earn more.

As young women we have limited ability to earn the cash we would like to have to fund our desires. Here is the Solution.

This CFO Training Manual will teach you Financial Planning Strategy Skills. Included are sections covering:

- Building a Budget with current Funds
- Delayed Gratification via Planning Purchases
- And Most Important-
- Identifying Interests & Building Skills to Develop a Small Business at Any Age

The management and entrepreneurial skills you learn at this age with this Training Manual will carry forward and benefit you the rest of your life.

Congratulations on allowing the Wise Woman's Academy to guide you on the path to your Best Self & Ideal Life.

Preview to the C F O Training

Train early to be the C.F.O. —
Chief Financial Officer — of your own life.
You're never too young to learn how to master
optimizing your money!

 Young people often have a limited ability to earn the cash they would like to have to fund their desires. Here is the Solution:

Learn to manage what you earn and how to earn more.

This CFO Training Manual will teach you Financial Planning Strategy Skills. Included are sections covering:

• Building a Budget with current Funds
• Delayed Gratification via Planning Purchases

And Most Important-

• Identifying Interests & Building Skills to Develop a Small Business at Any Age

The management and entrepreneurial skills you learn at this age with this Training Manual will carry forward and benefit you the rest of your life.

To some, "Millennial" means being born in a certain year or being a particular age.

However, in the Wise Woman's World, Millennial means being able to develop your favorite interests into skills that can help fund the lifestyle you want to live — sooner rather than later, or never.

Ready to have Abundance in Your Life?

Join US and learn how to structure the steps that lead to your Abundance of Time and Money.

Join The Wise Woman's Academy® and remember: knowledge and action are the keys to your financial success..

Congratulations on allowing the Wise Woman's Academy to guide you on the path to your Best Self & Ideal Life.

Preview to the CFO Training

Wise Bride – Wise Mommy & Wise Divorcee

Training early to be C. F. O. – Chief Financial Officer- of your own life puts YOU in the Driver's Seat to optimize your finances; current & future.

Look at life as a series of "Chapters" where we spend time on a defined path until we come to a fork in the road where we must choose our way. Every crossroad changes our experiences and circumstances. Some changes are for the better, some not as beneficial, and other changes are totally detrimental.

The life events covered in this volume of the Wise Woman's Academy program are pivotal financial points that can stabilize and enhance your mid-life and prime-life chapters or have ongoing negative financial implications that you may never fully recover from.

Planning a detailed strategy for your financial success as a Bride, Mommy or a Divorcee will yield tremendous life-long benefits, and make all future chapters much easier and very comfortable.

Congratulations on allowing the Wise Woman's Academy to guide you on the path to your Best Self & Ideal Life.

Intro to the CFO Training

Wise Businesswoman Funding the Next Step

Congratulations! As a Business Owner you had a Dream and worked extremely hard to make it a profitable reality.

So where do you go from here?

This Wise Woman's Academy C. F. O. Training Manual will transform you into a Savvy Financial Guru and show you the Best Strategy to Accumulate and Grow your Profits, risk free, and keep you from paying income taxes again and again on the same money.

Also included is help on Deciding the Next Step: to grow with more services or multiple locations and how to stop Client Loss by transforming your Best Employees into Partner Material with Buy in Cash.

Let's get started, a Dramatically Profitable Future is here at your fingertips.

Congratulations on allowing the Wise Woman's Academy to guide you on the path to your Best Self & Ideal Life.

Intro to the CFO Training

Wise Woman's Guide to Retirement Planning & Structuring Inheritance

Not preparing for your retirement yet?

If you're 30 or 40, it's definitely time to pad your savings and assure those accounts carry no risk of loss and minimal or no income taxes during your golden years.

If you're older than 30 or 40, it's not too late to start— just more costly. So start now!

This Wise Woman's Academy C.F.O. Training Manual has all the details on the Best No Risk, Tax Free Income Stream Plan plus additional information on exploring other financial considerations for this time of life such as:

- How long should you continue Working Full Time?
- When to start your Social Security Draw and why
- Details and Advantages of a Reverse Mortgage

This volume also includes important information on structuring inheritance gifts to your children and grandchildren so that all parties are happy and remain united and loving after the reading of your will.

Congratulations on allowing the Wise Woman's Academy to guide you on the path to your Best Self & Ideal Life.

References

- Table - Building a Million Dollar Retirement Account by David Bach
- Table – Comparison of Historical Performance of S&P 500 Index and IUL by Dan Aguayo
- The Million Dollar Baby IUL on YouTube to understand how compounding interest really works: (www.youtube.com/watch?v=jXIPwCpANO0)

- **Note:** The "Save Early Table" on page 45 & 46 and the "Save Later Table" on page 47 & 48 were found on Facebook. I am seeking the complete article as well as the Author's name so I can properly credit the information. If you have the missing info please contact me. Thank You.

For detailed information and the latest updates, contact me at:

jjnoccoauthor@gmail.com

Recommended Reading*

- The Retirement Miracle by Patrick Kelley

- Money. Wealth. Life Insurance by Jake Thompson

- Power of Zero by David McKnight

- Look Before You LIRP by David McKnight

- Pirates of Manhattan I & II by Barry Dyke

- 401(K)oas by Andy Tanner

- The 12 Week Year by Moran & Lennington